ROCKS AND ROCK COLLECTING

by EVA KNOX EVANS

GOLDEN PRESS · NEW YORK

Distributed by Crown Publishers, Inc.
419 Park Avenue South, N.Y., N.Y. 10016

EDITORIAL ADVISORS

JOSETTE FRANK, *Director for Children's Books,*
Child Study Association of America
DR. LELAND B. JACOBS, *Professor of Education,*
Teachers College, Columbia University

CREDITS

Cover: Gil Cohen
Illustrations: Raymond Perlman
Photographs: Anaconda, 46; British Information Service, 7; Paul Jensen, 30–31; Luray Caverns, 48; Josef Muench, 3, 8; National Geographic Society— "Folsom Hunters Spearing Bison" André Durenceau for the *National Geographic Magazine,* © National Geographic Society, Washington, D.C., 14; National Park Service, 9, 11; Rock of Ages Corp., 36; Hal Roth, 33; Bob and Ira Spring, 4, 27; Union Pacific Rail Road, 21; University of New Mexico, 17; Harold Wanless, 10

CONTENTS

The sea is constantly eroding our rocky shores.

Rocks Are Everywhere

ROCKS are everywhere. All of us see them so often we hardly notice them. In the country we pass by quarries, by cuts where new roads have been built, by old stone walls, by streams whose bottoms are covered with pebbles. Even on city pavements we often see a stone and kick it out of the way. An ordinary rock may seem to be the most uninteresting thing in the world.

But that is before you pick one up and really look at it. Held up to the light, the rock can sparkle and glisten with all sorts of tiny, bright-colored minerals that are hiding there. And that, too, is before you learn the exciting tales that rocks can tell.

A rock or pebble, picked up in a creek bed, on a sandy beach, or in an open field, tells something of the beginning of the world. It may tell of a high mountain far to the north that was ground down by great sheets of ice, and its stones and boulders carried by the moving ice to your own home town. A pebble can tell the story of a great volcano that blew its top millions of years ago, and scattered hot lava that hardened into stone.

Our whole earth is nothing more than a round, bumpy ball with a rock crust. Much of the crust is covered by water, but underneath the oceans and seas, rivers and lakes, there are rocks. Some of the ball is covered by great cities. The skyscrapers and subways, paved streets and apartment buildings all rest on a deep layer of rocks.

Green fields and tree-covered mountains, mucky swamps and hot deserts lie just above the rocky crust, and the soil from which plants grow is made of rocks. So the clothes we wear, the food we eat, the houses we live in, all began with the rocks that form the hard outside of our whirling earth.

The crust hasn't always been hard. At the very beginning the earth was just a spinning mass of burning, smoking lava— the same kind of lava that sometimes hisses and spits out of our active volcanoes. But gradually the outside began to stop burning and smoking. It cooled off. As it

Lava squeezed up through the earth's crust sometimes hardens into regular basalt columns.

cooled it hardened into the rocky crust. This hardened lava formed the first rocks of the world, and you can see them every day almost everywhere. They sometimes look quite slick and glassy, and sometimes you can see the grains in them.

They are called "igneous." The word means fire, and fire is certainly what these rocks had been before they cooled and became hard.

As the burning ball of the earth cooled, it didn't harden into anything very smooth.

Sedimentary layers are visible in these weathered sandstone cliffs.

There were great deep hollows in the round ball, and they filled with water.

All around and about the hollow places that formed the great seas and oceans, huge mountains of stone rose up. Wind and rain, ice and snow began to beat down on them and wear them down. Great boulders were carried from one place and put into another. Rain and ice ground the rocks into fine dirt and sand, which filled up the hollow places on the land, and

8

settled in the bottoms of the rivers, lakes and seas. As this sand and dirt piled layer on thick layer through the countless ages, it pressed into hard rocks again. You can find them everywhere. They are usually made up of the same kind of sand, sometimes brightly colored, and often there are pieces of plants or even fossils to be found in them.

These kinds of rocks are called "sedimentary." That's because any dust, dirt or sand that settles is called sediment.

Bones of ancient animals were trapped and preserved as sedimentary rock was forming.

Rocks piled on top of other rocks, as the earth shifted and changed. The rocks that were on the bottom were pressed down so that they didn't look like the same rocks that they were before. They began as sedimentary or igneous ones, but heat and water and time pressed them into another kind.

There is a long word for these kinds of rocks. It is "metamorphic." The word means change. You can find them, too, although they will be harder to recognize than the others.

Gneiss, a metamorphic rock,
is formed from igneous or sedimentary rock
under great heat and pressure.

Wind and rain eroded these lava formations.

Rocks to this very day keep changing and growing. There are a few volcanoes that still spit out their hot lava, and when it cools it forms igneous rock. Wind and rain pile up sand and dirt, which is pressed together into sedimentary ones. We don't feel it, but the rocky crust of the earth is constantly shifting and squeezing and changing, and so metamorphic rocks keep forming, too.

People who know the stories of stones have only to look at a piece of rock to tell what kind it is. If you are interested enough to look and learn, you, too, will be able to read their stories.

Using Rocks—
Yesterday and Today

AFTER the round, rocky ball had cooled off, man came to live on the earth. What did he find here? There were great mountains and deep valleys, great lakes and deep seas. There were swampy forests and dangerous animals lurking everywhere. Man also found rocks.

The earliest families crept into rocky caves to get away from the boiling sun and cold winds. They hid behind great boulders when enemies were near. When the first man learned to reach down and pick up a rock in his hand, he had learned the most useful thing of all. By throwing it he could kill an animal for his food or protect his life. He was much safer.

The first man who bound a stone onto a stick with a strong rope of animal skin had invented a tool. Now man had a hammer.

Some of the stones the early man found were sharp instead of round. When they tied one of these sharp-edged rocks to a

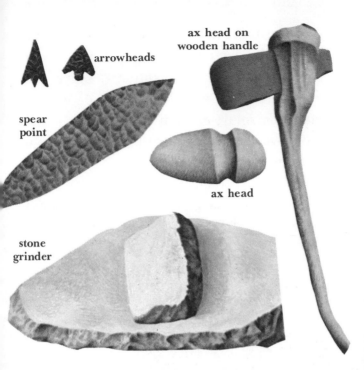

Early man's first tools were made of stones
shaped by nature. Later he learned to chip and
grind them to suit his needs.

stick, there was an ax—an ax that would
cut. They learned that some stones were
harder than other stones. With the hardest
ones they could cut and scrape and whittle
away on the softer ones and make
themselves a cutting tool.

All of this may seem very crude and silly to us, who have only to go to a hardware store to buy all the hammers, knives and axes we need. But if these early people had not been smart enough to make their stone tools, we might not have had the steel ones we have today.

The Indians of prehistoric North America killed giant bison with stone-tipped spears.

Because rocks and stones kept the ancient people alive, and because they were able to use them in many important ways, that first long period in the history of man has been named the Stone Age.

The Indians probably came to America during the time of the Stone Age. They brought their stone tools along with them. They invented some more, just as they were being invented in other parts of the world, too. Since the Indians used these tools up until the time the white men came, we know a great deal about them. They can still be found in places where Indians lived long ago.

They used sharp cutting stones for skinning animals and for scraping off the fur. They used round smooth stones for rubbing fat into these skins to make them soft enough to use for clothes, tepees and blankets. They didn't find out about iron that is to be found in some rocks, but they found obsidian, a very hard and glasslike stone. They used this for knives and chisels. The Mexican Indians split off large thin pieces of it for mirrors.

COPPER

GOLD

Copper and gold may be found in rocks
or as separate nuggets.

The Indians of the Americas also found
gold and copper — both minerals found in
rocks. With their stone tools they made
these metals into beautiful jewelry. The
Incas of South America even used gold for
cementing blocks of stones together to
build very special palaces for very special
kings. This gold, found in the earth or in
the beds of streams and rivers, was so
sparkly bright in the sunshine that the
word for gold in one of the Indian
languages meant "tears wept by the sun."

As soon as bows and arrows were invented, the Indians used a hard mineral called flint for the arrowheads. They cut and shaped the flint with other stones to make them just the right shape for killing a deer. They also discovered that this flint shot off sparks if it accidentally struck another rock. Then they knew how to start a fire.

It is certainly true that early man would not have survived if there had not been

Stone spearheads like these have been found lodged in the bones of ancient bison.

stones everywhere, and if he had not been smart enough to use them in all kinds of different ways to help make his life better. The Stone Age has been over for thousands and thousands of years. But that doesn't mean that we don't use rocks and minerals every day of our lives.

Look around and you can see stone buildings, crushed rock on our highways, sand in cement, stone walls and stone bridges. The salt on your table is the mineral halite. The chalk you use at school

Clay is a basic building material.

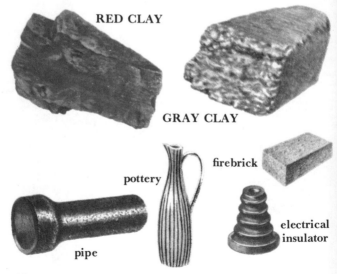

RED CLAY

GRAY CLAY

firebrick

pottery

pipe

electrical insulator

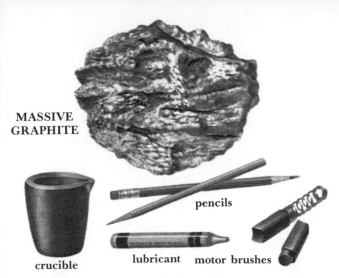

MASSIVE GRAPHITE

pencils

crucible   lubricant   motor brushes

Graphite, a soft mineral, is used in many ways.

is a soft-graincd limestone. The blackboard is a metamorphic rock-slate. The linoleum on your kitchen floor is probably made from copalite, a resin found in rocks.

The "lead" in our pencils is made from the mineral graphite. The oil for our cars and stoves comes from another mineral product, petroleum. Steel is made from iron, a mineral.

The gold ring on your finger, the jewel in your mother's earrings, the dime and nickel in your pocket all come from minerals—minerals found in stones. The list could go on and on.

Unusual Rocks

PICK up a handful of sand on the shore of some lake. If you look at it carefully you will notice that each grain may be a different color. Some rocks are made from sand. The wind and water and the pressures of other rocks have cemented the tiny grains into a hard stone, sandstone. Sometimes it's the other way around. The sands are only tiny grains from rocks worn away and loosened by the rain and wind. If you look, you may be able to find the mother rock that gave us each kind of mineral present in our sand.

Sand has also had a part in forming some peculiar looking rocks. Ancient hollow snail shells have filled up with sand and hardened into rock. Through the ages the shell has rotted or worn away and left a stone shaped with the whorls and pointed end of a snail.

In some of our western states, particularly Texas, rocks have been found shaped like corkscrews and imbedded in a larger piece of sandstone. These have been formed

The beautiful colors of Bryce Canyon's cliffs
come from oxides of iron and manganese present
in the sandstone and limestone rocks.

by some animal of long ago burrowing down through the stone and leaving a corkscrew hole. These holes filled with sand, which became cemented together into a twisted rock. They can be lifted out of the sandstone in one piece. Some have been found that are fifteen feet long and six inches in diameter, with the fossil remains of the animal that made the hole still inside them.

Balls of mud, almost round, have dried and formed rocks. As they dried, cracks formed, and sand sifted into the cracks and hardened. The sand was a different color from the hard mud ball, and the whole thing looks very much like a turtle.

Curious shapes, called concretions, sometimes form around a nucleus of sand or a fossil.

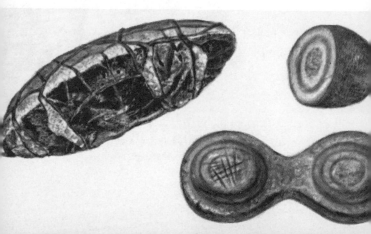

The weird shape above is a fulgerite,
formed when lightning struck sand and fused it
into a tube. Such tubes are usually
glassy on the inside.

Lightning sometimes strikes a wet sandy beach. The sudden heat fuses the sand into a tube — a tube you can blow through.

You will not find these curiously shaped rocks as easily as you can find a piece of sandstone or a grain of sand. But no matter what rock or pebble you pick up, you may be holding a real antique in your hands, an antique that is almost as old as the earth itself.

23

Some stones are more interesting than others. They are different shapes and colors, for one thing. All rocks are formed of minerals, and these minerals are formed of chemicals. The chemicals make the minerals look and act in most interesting ways.

There is hard shale, found in Brazil, that will burn if you put a lighted match to it. There is a rock called magnetite or lodestone which is really a magnet. It will pick up nails and other metal objects.

Certain types of rocks which appear to be quite ordinary contain surprises inside. Geodes are perhaps the most interesting, and they can be found in many places in the United States. When you pick up one of these rough, roundish stones, you may be surprised at how light it is. That's because it is nearly hollow inside. Geodes were once round or egg-shaped holes in clay or limestone. Water trickled into the hole. The tiny minerals dissolved in it hardened around the border of the hole, layer after layer. With wind and rain and changing earth, the clay or limestone that

This beautiful crystal of calcite formed inside
a geode along with smaller quartz crystals.

surrounded the geode was washed away,
leaving a hard mineral rock, almost hollow
inside, but lined with beautiful gemlike
crystals.

There have been geodes found along the banks of streams in Iowa partly filled with water that has not yet evaporated. Many are found in South America. Some geodes are made of agate, with precious crystals inside that are often used for jewelry. Some of these geodes are found in dry, barren places where there are no springs or streams to furnish water.

There are other hollow rocks with loose pebbles inside called "rattle boxes" because of the sound they make when you shake them. The Indian witch doctors used these to frighten sick people into getting well. And another hollow rock, called Indian Paint Pot, is filled with a reddish mineral, fine-grained as powder. Indians used this for their war paint.

Some sandstones, called Paint Pots, contain soft deposits of red or yellow iron ore.

This fossil leaf of an ancient ginko plant is embedded in shale.

There are other types of stones that are not hollow and not round with surprises inside. In Illinois, long, flat stones can be found that, split open, show leaves and bits of wood or even the imprint of insects that lived and grew in swampy places ages and ages ago.

There is one rock that doesn't have to be broken for you to see what is inside. This is amber, which is petrified resin from pine trees that lived millions of years ago. The resin oozed out of these trees and then hardened into stone. Sometimes a little

Long ago, this insect was trapped in resin which later hardened into amber.

insect became trapped in the sticky resin. Because amber is almost like glass you can see the ancient insect imbedded inside.

In Germany, along the Baltic sea, some amber is mined deep in the earth where the ancient trees have long since rotted away and left the petrified resin behind. But sometimes it is washed up out of the ocean where it can be picked up by some lucky person among pebbles and rocks on the beach.

Stone Forests
and Meteorites

MANY of you have traveled through Arizona and Wyoming and seen the petrified forests there. If you haven't been lucky enough to get there, you have seen pictures of them. These are huge rocks that look exactly like trees—bark, branches and all. Some of them are lying around in pieces as if they had been sawed off by a power saw, and left forgotten there. Looking at them, you can see the rings that show growth in a tree.

These trees are really rocks now, although once they were green and growing. Wind might have blown them over; forest fires could have killed them; and of course even in those times there were insects to harm them. Many of them decayed just where they fell. But some were picked up by floods or ancient swift-flowing rivers and were carried sometimes a hundred miles by the rushing water and buried in mud and silt.

Broken trunks of petrified prehistoric
trees cover the Arizona desert with their
beautiful, jewel-like colors.

Through the long ages water trickled
into the wood, and the water carried
minerals that were left behind in the tree.
It all happened so slowly, drop by drop,
that each tiny air cell in the wood was

replaced by the hard mineral. The looks weren't changed very much, but the trees became about 98 percent mineral and only about 2 percent wood.

This mineral was usually quartz, which is often white or gray. Other minerals, too, seeped into the cracks and pores of the trees and gave them color. Sometimes these cracks are lined with beautiful opal or amethyst crystals.

Petrified wood weighs about 166 pounds a cubic foot. The chunks of logs look as if some giant saw had cut them into pieces just right for a fireplace. They were probably cracked by great earthquakes while the petrified trees were still buried in the mud. At first these cracks were very small, but hundreds of years later when the mud had been washed away and the logs were exposed to the air and rain, the cracks widened and finally broke through. Sometimes soil washed out from underneath one end of a log, and the weight made it sag and break.

The Indians found these pieces of petrified wood when they came here. The Arizona Indians were farmers and stayed in one place, building themselves sturdy houses. These houses were usually built of sandstone, but sometimes the Indians used pieces of petrified wood for building material because of the beautiful colors.

These majestic sandstone dwellings at Mesa Verde, Colorado, were built by prehistoric Indians.

One of these houses, called Agate House, in the Petrified Forest in Arizona, has been partly restored, using chunks of petrified wood which were found on the ruins of the original house.

The West is not the only place where petrified wood can be found. Nearly every state and some foreign countries have examples of it. Someday you may be surprised to find some near your own home.

Perhaps the strangest rocks found on the earth are the ones that once sailed through the sky. Meteors are usually called "shooting stars" and we often see their bright streak trailing across the sky on a summer night. Of course, they aren't stars at all, for stars are bodies as large as our sun and shine from a distance of billions of miles away.

Meteors are chunks of rock and iron sailing around out in space. Some of these chunks may be parts of comets that broke up. Others may be left over from materials torn from the sun, and they have been whirling around it for about three billion years. Every once in a while these whirling hunks of matter come close enough to the earth to be pulled by its gravity. They come speeding toward the earth at from twenty-five to eighty miles a second. As soon as the meteors come inside the earth's atmosphere—a hundred miles or so up in the sky—the friction of the air heats them until they glow. That's why we can see their light as they shoot across the sky. Most meteors burn up while they are still in the air. But sometimes these rocks come hurtling to earth. Those that land are called meteorites. Some of them have been found weighing hundreds of tons, but many are no larger than an orange. If you should ever come across one you have found something almost as valuable as a jewel.

This meteorite has been cut in two, and a surface polished to show its metallic structure.

Looking for Rocks

PERHAPS you are interested and curious enough to pick up a rock and really look at it. You may even take it home with you so you can study it some more. Then the next time you see another, different-looking rock, you pick it up and take it home, too. Before you know it, you have started a rock collection. You have a hobby.

If you live in the country or a small town you won't have any trouble finding some rocks. But even if you live in the city where sidewalks and buildings take up most of the space, there are still places where you can pick up some stones.

Building sites are good places to look for rocks. Bulldozers, digging deep into the earth, bring up all kinds of rocks. There may be quarries, iron smelters, or mines nearby where you can find specimens. Factories that make granite and marble monuments may be glad to give you chips they don't need.

This huge granite quarry in Vermont has supplied stone for hundreds of buildings.

Perhaps you go to a summer camp. You will have plenty of chances there to add to your collection. A hike with the Scouts, a picnic at a beach, a trip with your family in the summer—all give you a chance to find good samples of rocks if you keep your eyes open.

The first rocks in your collection will be the ones you find in your own neighborhood. They are not always the same everywhere. If you live in New York, the rocks you find in your back yard will be very different from the rocks you would find if you lived in Colorado.

Granite and sandstone are two common rocks found in many places in the United States. If you have a piece of granite, look at it carefully, for you will see small pieces

Sandstone from New York, left, is coarser than the dark red sandstone from Utah.

MEDIUM-GRAINED GRANITE

quartz

feldspar

biotite mica

FINE-GRAINED GRANITE

RED GRANITE

Granite is a hard igneous rock made up of a mixture of several crystalline minerals.

of glassy, rough-edged grains, looking something like tiny pieces of broken glass. That is quartz. There may be some yellowish grains, with each grain broken into flat shiny surfaces that reflect the light. That is feldspar. In between the quartz and feldspar there will be dark particles quite different from the other two. These flake off in thin sheets, and that is mica.

39

All rocks are made of minerals. You can't collect one without collecting the other. Suppose you make some chocolate fudge. You mix sugar and cocoa, milk and butter, vanilla and perhaps a pinch of salt. You cook it and then set it aside to harden. It is fudge, but it is also a blend of all the things you put into it.

In the same way, rocks are a blend of different minerals, sometimes many, sometimes just a few.

If you put pecans in your fudge, they would not blend with the sugar, milk and cocoa unless you ground them up first. Sometimes one special mineral doesn't get blended in the rock, either, and you notice it just as you can see the nuts in fudge.

The rock that holds this special mineral is called a matrix. Some of the minerals found in rocks are precious stones like diamonds, rubies and sapphires. You probably won't find any of these lying along the roadside. But there are other beautiful crystals and metals to be found in ordinary looking rocks if you are careful when you are collecting them. Remember

Garnets, left, and emeralds may be
found in a matrix of schist.

that the matrix, or rock, that holds the
mineral can be just as interesting as the
mineral itself.

Sometimes, you can find a beautiful
piece of quartz or garnet all by itself. That
means that the rock matrix has been worn
away by water, wind and weather, leaving
the harder mineral behind. If you should
put a piece of chocolate pecan fudge into
some water, the blend of cocoa, milk,
sugar, salt, butter and vanilla would be
washed away and the piece of pecan would
be left all alone. That is what has
happened when you find a piece of milky
quartz or dark red garnet all by itself.

When you start out on a collecting trip,
you will need a little special equipment

41

besides good sturdy legs and a sharp eye. You may see a very high cliff with interesting pale pink bands running through the rocks. You can't take the whole cliff home—yet you want a piece of this rock for your collection.

You will need a hammer. Supply houses sell a special hammer for this purpose which is flat on one end and sharp-pointed on the other. But if you can't afford to get one of these, you can use a plasterer's or bricklayer's hammer. The kind a carpenter uses is not quite strong enough for hard stone. You will give a sharp tap to a piece of that cliff, and then use the sharp end to pry it off.

It may not come away easily, so use a cold chisel. This can be bought at a hardware store or perhaps your father has one that he will lend you. Insert the chisel in the crack, and tap it with your hammer, gradually working a small piece of stone loose from the larger rock.

Then you may want to scrape the surface dirt off so you can see what you really have. Use your pocket knife for this job.

A pocket magnifying glass is a handy thing to have along on a collecting trip. The magnifying glass may show up some minerals you didn't know were there. If you don't look at your rocks carefully, you may throw away something valuable.

You never know how many rocks you will find in an afternoon, so take along a knapsack or a heavy leather bag for carrying them back home. Arrange it so you can sling it across your back. It's much more convenient when you're hiking or climbing to have both arms free.

Take some newspapers along so that you can wrap each specimen separately. Many of them might have precious minerals in them that could get damaged if they're

The right equipment makes collecting easier and more rewarding.

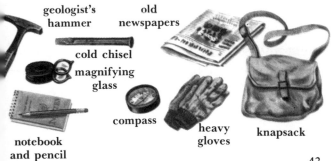

geologist's hammer

old newspapers

cold chisel

magnifying glass

compass

notebook and pencil

heavy gloves

knapsack

43

Specimens collected on a field trip
should be wrapped individually, with a note
telling where you found them.

knocked about. Tear the paper into quarter
sheets, put the rock in the center and fold
the sides and then the ends to make a neat
package.

While you are hunting for rocks you
may come across a beautiful sheet of mica,
or a fine piece of quartz. These are delicate
and need special handling. They can be
smashed to smithereens if you just wrap
them and put them in the bag with the rest
of your rocks. A box with some cotton in it
is a safe way to carry delicate samples.

Perhaps you have found a pocket of
beautifully colored sands that would be

44

interesting to keep. Small bottles can be useful. Test tubes are ideal for this, but clean aspirin or other pill bottles are just as good and cost nothing.

Don't wait to begin collecting until you have all the equipment. Keep your eyes open for any rock or pebble that might seem interesting. Pick it up and take it home with you. Once it is washed and really clean it might mean an important addition to your collection. You never know where one will turn up.

Here is a reminder of the things that can be useful on a collecting trip:

1. Mineralogist's hammer, for breaking off a sample.
2. Cold chisel, for prying sample loose.
3. Magnifying glass, for seeing what you have.
4. Knapsack, for carrying samples home.
5. Newspapers, for wrapping.
6. Pen knife, for cleaning.
7. Old gloves, so that you won't cut your hands.
8. Cotton, boxes and bottles, for carrying delicate minerals.

If you're interested in rocks, you have a new name. You're a "rockhound." A rockhound is a person who hunts for rocks and minerals, always looking for something different, something interesting, something beautiful.

Up to now you may have been collecting along a roadside. Maybe you have only had to walk down the road to a gravel pit or walk out on the shores of a lake or the sea. But you will want as many different kinds of rocks and minerals as you can get.

A mine is a good place to look for rocks for your collection.

Mines, quarries and monument works can give you a chance to collect some of these fairly near home.

A visit to one of these places is very different from a trip to a cliff by the side of the road. In the first place, you must get permission. If the quarry is near by, ask for the superintendent when you go there, tell him what you want to do, and ask if he will let you visit. If the quarry is far from home and someone must drive you there, it would be better to write a letter to the company first.

Address your letter to the superintendent. Be sure to tell him that an adult will be with you, and ask for permission to visit, and the most suitable time to come. It might be a good idea to enclose a stamped self-addressed envelope with your letter.

When you are collecting there is no need to take home a lot of samples of the same kind of rock or mineral. But it is a good idea to take several of each kind if you find some interesting ones. You can use these later for trading.

Stalacites and stalagmites form in limestone caves.

If You're a Rockhound

ONCE you have collected a specimen of each local rock, you won't want to stop there. You may want a coral geode from Florida, a piece of pink marble from Georgia, a stalactite from one of the Virginia caves and a piece of petrified wood from Wyoming. How do you go about getting them if you don't live anywhere near?

One of the easiest ways is to buy them. You won't need too much money as a beginning, for sometimes one dollar will buy some very interesting specimens. There

48

are regular supply houses that sell rocks and minerals. Many of them send free catalogues with price lists. You can search through these to find the specimens you need at a price you can afford.

If you swap, you will want to be sure that your rocks are very special because you can't swap something ordinary for something extraordinary. The samples you have must be valuable enough for someone else to want. It wouldn't make sense to offer to send a rockhound in New Hampshire a piece of granite. His back yard is probably full of it.

You must also know where the specimens you particularly want can be found. There is no use writing the same rockhound that you will swap him a piece of pink marble for a piece of petrified wood. He might need the marble, but he probably couldn't find an inch of petrified wood in all of New Hampshire.

The next step is to find other collectors ready to swap with you. Rock collecting can be a lot more fun if you know others who have the same hobby. By this time your best friend may be a rockhound, too. Perhaps the two of you could get together with some of your friends and exchange specimens and ideas about getting some more. There are often mineral clubs at museums or libraries that you can join.

If you belong to the Scouts, your troop leader may help you. You can get a merit badge for a rock and mineral collection. This may be a fine way to get in touch with other Scouts in other states who may be rockhounds, too.

There are a hundred or so mineral clubs scattered over the country in many of our cities and large towns. Grown-ups belong to these clubs, but they will be glad to help you in any way they can to give you a good start on your mineral hobby.

If you don't know anyone else who is a rockhound and you can't seem to get anyone else interested, don't be discouraged. You're not really alone. There are always the mails. Many magazines published especially for young people have letter columns, and some of them have swap departments. You could write a letter and send it to one of these magazines saying what your hobby is and asking other people interested in rocks to write to you. Or you could write to the "swap column" telling what you have to swap and what you would like to get in return.

If you come across something that is really unusual, you may want to put an ad in one of the rocks and minerals magazines. Advertisements like these should be carefully worded, telling exactly what your specimen is like. Be sure that what you have to swap is as valuable as the stone you want to get in return. When you are mailing rock or mineral specimens, they must be wrapped as carefully as delicate china. Minerals can get scratched and rocks can be chipped unless they are wrapped in newspapers and packed so that they won't jostle around in the box.

Once you begin writing letters to other people interested in rocks, you may be corresponding with a real expert on the subject—a museum director, or a writer of books on minerals, a college professor or an engineer.

Rocks can be stored neatly in a divided box.

Rock Collections

THE specimens you have carefully collected need to be stored in a special place. That is the only way you can enjoy them. Arranging your collection in the best possible way can be as much fun as collecting the stones.

Cigar boxes make good storage places until you can arrange something more permanent. Your corner drugstore will be glad to give you some. Divide each one with heavy cardboard or strips of plywood, to separate the specimens.

Eventually you will want a cabinet for your collection. In the attic, or perhaps in a secondhand store, you may find an old bookcase or china cabinet. The ones with glass doors are best.

Some collectors have tiers of drawers which pull out to show trays of their rocks and minerals. The supply houses sell these. A secondhand chest of drawers or an old filing case or spool cabinet can be used just as well. Then you will be ready to arrange your collection. First of all, each rock should be washed well with warm water. Do not use soap—it may make a film on the surface of your stone. Scrape a fresh surface with your knife, or break one with your mineral hammer. Do this carefully for you will not want to break off any of the shiny mineral grains or crystals that are showing. Then polish with a dry cloth.

Many collectors like to mount their specimens on a small block of wood so they will show off better. Some museums carve a nest in the wood just the right shape for the bottom of the rock or mineral so that it will rest there securely. But if you are not an expert woodcarver it will be better for you to use glue. Put a little dab of household cement in the middle of your block of wood and press the rock or mineral firmly on that. Be sure to select the most interesting side for showing. Don't move it for a day or two so that the cement will have time to harden. Your collection will look neater if each wood block is exactly the same size and shape.

Your specimens are now ready to be labeled. If you are storing them on shelves, you could place a card with the name of the specimen in front of each. But cards sometimes get separated from their specimens, and so most collectors use numbers and a notebook.

Let's suppose that you have a piece of granite with a large bright crystal of quartz imbedded in it and its number is 17. Then in a notebook you will write something like this:

17. Granite with clear quartz crystal. Found in Little Rock Quarry, Little Rock, Arkansas. Mr. Charles Brown, Superintendent.

You can add other things about this particular rock. Perhaps you traded it. If you did, write the name of the person and his address, and what you sent him in exchange. You may want to write to him again and do some more swapping. Or you may have found this piece of quartz yourself. Then, of course, you will write where you found it and any other interesting things connected with the adventure.

A small piece of adhesive tape with the number printed on it can be used to identify each rock, but it's not the neatest way. Eventually, the adhesive will begin to curl at the edges and may come off.

The best way is to select a smooth place on the surface of the rock. Pick out a spot that won't interfere with the looks of it. Take some white enamel paint and a tiny paintbrush and make a neat round dot about the size of an aspirin tablet. After

You can label your rocks with paint and ink.

No. _41_   Date _9/13/65_
Name _Hematite_
Locality _Rome, N.Y._
Collector _H.S. Zim_

The records and notes you keep may turn out to be as important as the specimens you collect.

the white paint dries, write the number on the white spot with India ink. If you do it this way you will always have a number on the specimen. It isn't as easy as it sounds. The paint can streak and run, and ruin the looks of your collection. Practice on a rock that you don't want to keep until you're sure you know how to do it.

Keeping a notebook may be a chore if you're not very fond of writing. But your collection will not be nearly as interesting or valuable unless you do. Rocks and minerals stored neatly and labeled carefully can give you pleasure for a lifetime.

Identifying Rocks

You remember that a rock collector should be a good detective. Scientists have worked for years classifying and naming the rocks and minerals of this old earth and they haven't finished yet. But if you find a rock or mineral you will certainly want to know what it is. There are certain clues you can follow.

One of them is color. At first, that doesn't seem too hard, for all of us can look at something and tell what it looks like. With minerals, though, it's a little harder than you think. Sometimes minerals get mixed up with materials that don't belong to them and these materials can change the color.

Quartz is colorless and clear. The ancient men who found it thought it was ice frozen so hard it wouldn't melt. But you may find quartz in almost all the colors of the rainbow, plus milky white and brown and black. The color isn't supposed to be there. Impurities, sometimes just mud, get mixed in with the clear crystal. You could mistake

ROSE QUARTZ

QUARTZ AMETHYST

SMOKY QUARTZ

BLUE QUARTZ

**SMOKY QUARTZ
(MORION FORM)**

CITRINE QUARTZ

MILKY QUARTZ

Sometimes it is hard to recognize a rock or
mineral by its color. For instance, quartz may
be found in several colors, as shown here.

quartz for something else if color were the
only test you could use. Often only the
surface of a mineral is discolored. If you
carefully scrape off the outside layer, the
true color will be there underneath.

The streak test is another way of
identifying some minerals by color. Get a
piece of unglazed porcelain. The rough
back of a section of tile, like the kind that
may line your bathroom wall, makes a
good streak plate. Rub your mineral across
that. The color made on the porcelain by
the streak may be different from the
mineral itself.

For instance, the mineral pyrite looks
yellow, but it makes a black streak. It

The streak test is a way of identifying some minerals. Here, streak is not the same color as the mineral.

always makes a black streak on porcelain. Yellow quartz won't make a black streak— only pyrite will, so if you have a yellow mineral you're not quite sure about, test it this way.

Another clue is hardness. Each type of mineral has a certain degree of hardness. This has nothing to do with how easily it can be broken. It's really a scratching test.

Ten minerals have been set up by the scientists against which all the other minerals can be tested for hardness:

1. Talc	6. Orthoclase
2. Gypsum	7. Quartz
3. Calcite	8. Topaz
4. Fluorite	9. Corundum
5. Apatite	10. Diamond

Talc, as number one, is the softest. Diamond, as number ten, is the hardest.

It works like this: quartz has a hardness of 7. It will scratch orthoclase (no. 6) but it will not scratch topaz (no. 8). If you find a mineral that will scratch quartz and yet it will not scratch topaz, you know that the mineral has a hardness of between 7 and 8.

Rock and mineral supply houses sell these sets of hardness minerals, and it would be a fine thing if you could buy a set. But there is another way to test for hardness which doesn't cost a penny. It is not quite as accurate but it will give you a good idea of the hardness of your mineral.

Talc and gypsum (nos. 1 and 2) can be scratched with your fingernail. Any mineral that can be scratched that way has a hardness of between 1 and 2.

Calcite can be scratched by a penny. Test the mineral with a one cent piece, and

Hardness is another test that can be used in mineral identification.

Try to scratch A with B

Try to scratch B with A

A scratches B

B does not scratch A

if it can be scratched that way, and yet not with your fingernail, it has a hardness of 3.

Fluorite (no. 4) can be easily scratched by a knife but a penny won't make a mark on it.

Apatite (no. 5) can just barely be scratched with the knife.

Orthoclase (no. 6) will scratch your knife blade instead of the other way around. Any mineral that can do that will have a hardness of at least 6.

Quartz (no. 7) will scratch a piece of glass, but topaz (no. 8) will scratch the quartz. Corundum will scratch topaz, and diamond is the hardest of all and will scratch almost anything. You won't have to worry too much about the last three minerals, though, because quartz is about

You can test many minerals for hardness simply by using a fingernail or the objects below.

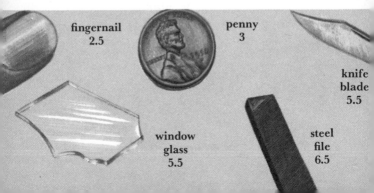

fingernail
2.5

penny
3

knife
blade
5.5

window
glass
5.5

steel
file
6.5

as hard a mineral as you will ever be able to find.

Does it sound difficult? It isn't really, if you practice a little. You may want to write down the hardness of each of your minerals in your notebook. If you use your fingernail, a penny, your knife and a piece of glass, you can give the hardness test while you're on a collecting trip.

Another way to test minerals is to see how they break. This is rather tricky business and takes a lot of practice before you tap one of your precious specimens with a hammer. Many minerals break into certain patterns no matter how hard they are hit. Even if a certain mineral is shattered into a thousand tiny pieces, each little piece will have exactly the same shape.

For instance, mica always breaks off in thin sheets. If you have a block of mica, you can split off a sheet of it with your knife if you do it carefully. Halite and galena break into cubes. If you strike a piece of galena with a hammer, the smaller pieces will look like tiny cubes, and the

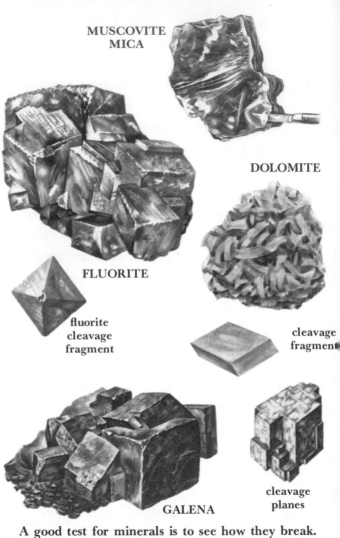

MUSCOVITE MICA

DOLOMITE

FLUORITE

fluorite
cleavage
fragment

cleavage
fragment

cleavage
planes

GALENA

A good test for minerals is to see how they break.
Some minerals split along planes into regular
patterns. These breaks are called cleavages.

larger pieces will look like a solid block built of a lot of tiny cubes. Fluorite breaks up into particles that have eight smooth sides. These kinds of regularly shaped breaks are called *cleavages*.

Some minerals do not break with a flat surface, as mica and galena and fluorite do. Quartz and obsidian break with a smooth rounded surface like a seashell. Copper breaks with rough, irregular and jagged edges. Some break into sharp, splintery pieces. These kinds of breaks are called *fractures*.

Of course you wouldn't want to try this test on your most beautiful specimen of quartz or mica unless you were very sure that you wouldn't smash it to smithereens.

The surest way to identify a mineral is by chemical tests. All minerals are made

Other minerals break into irregular shapes.
These breaks are called fractures.

OBSIDIAN   **ARSENOPYRITE**   **CLAY**

up of chemicals. The tests are made by adding other chemicals to the minerals to see what reaction they produce.

For instance, when acid is dropped on a mineral and the mineral bubbles, that is one way of knowing that it is a carbonate. If it smells like rotten eggs, that shows there is sulphur in the mineral.

Heating the mineral in a very hot flame is another way to identify it. The color of the mineral when heated may change, and show you the chemicals in it. Other tests depend on the fact that small amounts of

Your science teacher can help you test powdered minerals by heating them in closed and open tubes.

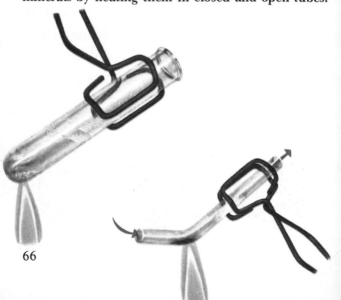

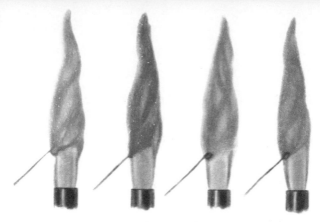

Another test requiring help and special equipment is the flame test. A flame will change color depending on the metals a mineral contains.

mineral put into a flame on the end of a special wire will color the flame.

These chemical and heat tests take some equipment that is sometimes dangerous to use. If you are very anxious to see these experiments perhaps your science teacher at school will help you.

You may be lucky enough to come across a very special kind of rock or mineral. You may not be able to identify it even after all the tests. If there is a museum in your town or a college, don't hesitate to take it there to see what they think of it. "Rocks and Minerals" magazine will help you, too, if you write to the editor.

Special Collections

IF YOU ever collected bottle caps, postal cards or pictures of baseball players, there was sure to come a time when you decided you had enough. Once you had as many or more than your friends you just weren't interested anymore.

That kind of thing doesn't happen to a rockhound. If you hunted for a lifetime you would probably never get a specimen of every kind of rock and mineral in the world. You will never be bored with your collection because there are too many interesting things to find out about it.

A specialized collection of rocks is harder to make than a collection of all kinds. But because it is difficult, it is much more fun. Each rock you find for your collection is far more exciting, far more important. Maybe you will have to wait a long time, and suddenly you have the one rock or mineral you've been wanting all along—as a present under the Christmas tree, or better still, you may find it yourself when you least expect it.

Fossils are not easy to find, but they make an
especially interesting collection. At the left
are trilobite fossils; at right, a fern leaf.

No one but you can decide what your
special collection will be. You might make
a collection of all the rocks and minerals
found in your own state. Fossil rocks, that
show the imprint of leaves or fish or
insects, or even a dinosaur's foot, thousands and thousands of years old, can make
an interesting special collection.

Perhaps Indian relics would be a good
one. You might collect a piece of flint or
quartz or copper-bearing stone, with an

FLINT   arrowhead   CHERT

You may want to collect stones used by the Indians.

arrowhead made from each. There are
many stones used for jewelry that can be
found in quarries near you or swapped
with your rockhound friends. Agates,
garnets, beryl, jasper, milky and colored
quartz are beautiful to look at and are not
hard to get.

Gemstones make a beautiful collection.

BANDED AGATE

JASPER

GARNET

BERYL

twinned
crystals

BARITE
"Desert Rose"

STAUROLITE

Another interesting speciality is odd-shaped rocks.

You may be most interested in the odd-shaped rocks and minerals, those that mimic something else. Some people collect sand and other microscopic minerals. They make a good collection, especially if you have a microscope.

There are many ways that you can use a good rock collection. It can make a special project for your science class at school, or you can exhibit it at a science fair if your city or county has one.

You may want to do some demonstrations in connection with your exhibit. You can make a compass. One variety of magnetite called lodestone acts as a magnet and has a north and south pole. A piece of lodestone can be your compass. Find the

71

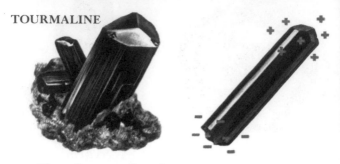

TOURMALINE

Heated tourmaline developes electric charges.

poles by dipping the lodestone in iron filings or some magnetite sand. The tiny filings will cling most thickly at the poles. Then tie a string around the middle of the lodestone between the poles, and let it hang freely in the air. It will twirl a little and then come to rest with the poles pointing north and south. Put a straw from a broom between the lodestone and the string for your compass needle.

Tourmaline also has positive and negative poles although it is not magnetic. You can prove this by heating a tourmaline crystal very carefully on a hot plate. One end of the crystal will then attract tiny pieces of paper, and that is the positive pole. The other end will repel the paper and that is the negative pole.

Another experiment takes longer but it shows how mineral crystals form. Boil a cup of water. Then dissolve about an ounce piece of rock salt (halite) in it. When it is dissolved, pour this liquid into a saucer and hang a piece of string in it with one end resting over the edge of the saucer. Put it in the sun or near a stove or radiator, and leave it for a few days. The water will slowly evaporate, and a coating of tiny crystals will be left on the string and the sides of the saucer. Look at them under a magnifying glass. You will see that each tiny crystal is shaped like a cube.

Halite occurs in cubic crystals and in compact masses called rock salt.

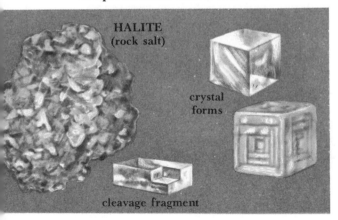

HALITE
(rock salt)

crystal
forms

cleavage fragment

Crystals of sugar, borax, washing soda and epsom salts can also be made in the same way for an experiment at home or at school. These crystals will not be cube-shaped, but they are all different and very interesting to see under a magnifying glass.

A really good special collection can make some money for you. Other rockhounds are in the market for unusual items. You may find something so rare that a museum may need it for its collection.

The scientists who make it their life's work to study and discover all they can about rocks and minerals are called geologists. They teach geology in our colleges and universities, write books, and are on the staffs of our museums.

Geologists are also employed by mining companies and oil companies. They take samples of sands and test and study them in their laboratories to discover what kind of rocks lie deep underground. Then they know whether oil or precious minerals are likely to be found in a certain area if they drill there.

STAR SAPPHIRE   RUBY   TOPAZ

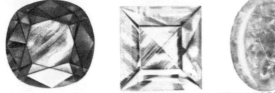

SMOKY QUARTZ ROCK CRYSTAL PRECIOUS OPAL

MALACHITE   LAPIS-LAZULI   MOONSTONE

Jewelers and gem-cuttters are rockhounds,
too. They specialize in precious, semi-precious,
and ornamental stones like these.

Jewelers and cutters of precious stones
are rockhounds, too. The shape of a rough
diamond shows the stone cutter how it
should be properly cut to make it more
sparkling and bright. The color and shape
of a garnet, an opal or an emerald shows
the artist how to design beautiful jewelry.
They are always on the lookout for different
kinds of stones, to make different kinds of
rings, bracelets and necklaces.

75

An interest in rocks can lead you to be a sculptor. The earliest pieces of sculpture must surely have been made by a rockhound. He found a stone that was shaped like a crouching lion, for instance. With a crude tool, he flaked off some in one place, a little off in another, and he had a statue of a lion. Our modern sculptors have to know about rocks, for often the color or texture of a rock suggests the kind of piece they want to carve: soapstone for one kind, granite for something entirely different.

Perhaps you may want to make jewelry or a piece of sculpture from some rocks or minerals you have collected. Cutting the hard gemlike minerals takes some special tools and some special learning. But there are handicraft classes you can join where you can use your beautiful rocks in all kinds of useful and attractive ways.

But even if you don't become a geologist, a sculptor, a miner or an artist in jewelry, your rock collection can give you pleasure for the rest of your life. A rockhound hardly ever stops being a rockhound.

"X" Marks the Spot

HERE are some of the more important rocks, minerals and metals found in each state.

Alabama: hematite, black copper, barite, muscovite, iron.

Alaska: gold, silver, copper, mercury, tungsten, magnetite.

Arizona: petrified wood, copper, silver, gold, amethyst, malachite, azurite, augite.

AUGITE

Arkansas: quartz crystals, garnet, manganese, yellow smithsonite, rutile, galena.

California: gold, silver, diamond, galena, barite, cinnabar, borax, garnet, gypsum, agate, carnelian, talc.

Colorado: galena, smoky quartz, topaz, aquamarine, orthoclase, garnet, copper, gold, silver, pyrite, uraninite, shale.

TOPAZ

Connecticut: barite, beryl, tourmaline, garnet, feldspar, mica, rutile, topaz.

Delaware: garnet, beryl, apatite, black tourmaline, loose quartz crystals.

GARNET

Florida: coral geodes, limestone, silicified shells.

Georgia: hematite, gold, fire opal, quartz, rutile, lazulite, chalcopyrite, granite, marble.

QUARTZ

Hawaii: lava rock, black coral, bauxite.

LAVA ROCK

Idaho: placer gold, pyrite, copper, opals, quartz, silver, basalt.

Illinois: shale, geode, illite, witherite, fluorite, greenockite, galena.

Indiana: "oolitic" limestone, halloysite.

Iowa: gypsum, aragonite, limestone, galena.

ARAGONITE

Kansas: zinc, lead, gypsum, galena.

Kentucky: geodes of quartz, gypsum rosettes, fluorite, pyrite, stalactites and stalagmites.

Louisiana: rock salt, gypsum, sulphur.

Maine: beryl, green and black tourmaline, cinnamon and yellow garnet, pyrite, fluorite, rose quartz, green mica, galena, feldspar, apatite.

PYRITE

Maryland: copper, smoky quartz, chlorite, marble, black tourmaline, magnetite, mica.

Massachusetts: rutile, mica, pyrite, beryl, feldspar, garnet, agate, apatite, asbestos, graphite, talc.

AGATE

Michigan: alabaster, gypsum, calcite, amethyst, quartz, copper.

Minnesota: hematite, geodes, agate, iron, magnetite, copper, orthoclase, gabbro.

HEMATITE

Mississippi: calcite, limestone.

Missouri: limestone, tripoli, rhyolite porphyry, chert, hematite, sandstone, diaspore, hemimorphite, wolframite, galena.

CALCITE

Montana: gold, sapphire, wood opal, silver, garnet.

Nebraska: clay, sandstone, limestone.

Nevada: silver, galena, gold, limestone, copper, obsidian, slate, igneous rocks mixed with granite.

New Hampshire: granite, beryl, mica, tourmaline, garnet, muscovite, quartz, graphite, garnet, soapstone, rutile in quartz, galena, mica, fluorite.

New Jersey: zinc, magnetite, apatite, tourmaline, calcite, fluorite, talc, copper, milky quartz, pyrite.

New Mexico: limestone, shale, turquoise, silver, gold, aragonite, amethyst, malachite.

New York: dolomite, magnetite, feldspar, zircon, tourmaline, apatite, limestone, garnet, graphite, basalt (Trap Rock), calcite, mica, talc, galena, pyrite.

BIOTITE
MICA

North Carolina: slate, gold in quartz, iron, magnetite, mica, beryl, emerald, garnet, orthoclase, talc.

North Dakota: lignite.

Ohio: gypsum, rock salt, alum, sulphur, calcite, fluorite.

Oklahoma: marcasite, dolomite, calcite, barite, galena, sphalerite.

BARITE

Oregon: gold, cinnabar, pyrite, nickel-iron, malachite, azurite, basalt, agate.

Pennsylvania: magnetite, galena, copper, nickel, smoky quartz, zircon, graphite, green mica, sunstone, limestone, yellow and white tourmaline, asbestos, slate.

SLATE

Rhode Island: amethyst, feldspar, magnetite, manganese, talc, graphite.

South Carolina: gold, zircon, tourmaline, magnetite, rutile, phosphate.

TOURMALINE

South Dakota: gold, tin, mica, feldspar, uraninite, beryl.

Tennessee: zinc, calamine, limonite, gypsum, alum, fluorite, marble.

Texas: calcite, limestone, "balls" of iron ore, sulphur.

Utah: sandstone, volcanic rocks, limestone, silver, galena, fossil plants sometimes replaced by silver, shale.

Vermont: marble, pyrite, garnet, mica, feldspar, quartz, tourmaline, slate, asbestos.

Virginia: limonite, zinc, quartz, gold, stalactites and stalagmites.

Washington: fire opal, quartz, tourmaline, some lead and silver minerals, basalt.

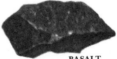

BASALT

West Virginia: blue celestite, limestone, hematite.

Wisconsin: galena, zinc, smithsonite, fossil ore, barite, calcite, pyrite, quartzite.

Wyoming: petrified wood, amethyst, quartz, geyserite, agate.

79

INDEX

Asterisk (*) indicates illustration